Why Do Fish Have Gills?

And Other Questions About Evolution and Classification

PAT JACOBS

PowerKiDS press

Published in 2017 by
The Rosen Publishing Group, Inc.
29 East 21st Street, New York, NY 10010

Cataloging-in-Publication Data
Names: Jacobs, Pat.
Title: Why do fish have gills? / Pat Jacobs.
Description: New York : PowerKids Press, 2017. | Series: Wildlife wonders | Includes index.
Identifiers: ISBN 9781499432060 (pbk.) | ISBN 9781499432398 (library bound) | ISBN 9781508153351 (6 pack)
Subjects: LCSH: Fishes--Juvenile literature.
Classification: LCC QL617.2 J33 2017 | DDC 597--d23

Copyright © 2017 Franklin Watts, a division of Hachette Children's Group

Series Editor: Julia Bird
Packaged by: Dynamo Limited

Picture credits
Key: **t**=top, **b**=bottom, **l**=left, **r**=right.
Cover: cbpix/Shutterstock, bluehand/Shutterstock, Andrey_Kuzmin/Shutterstock, p1 cbpix/Shutterstock; p3 bluehand/Shutterstock; p4 **t** wanchai/Shutterstock, p4 **b** littlesam/Shutterstock; p5 **t** pelena/Shutterstock, p5 **b** Catmando/Shutterstock; p6 lungfish Tatiana Volgutova/Shutterstock, p6 eel picturepartners/Shutterstock, p6 flatfish Kristina Vackova/Shutterstock; p7 perch Joana Milanko/Shutterstock, p7 sea dragon tristan tan/Shutterstock, p7 lantern fish Phil Jacobs, p7 stickleback Krasowit/Shutterstock, p7 herring shoal Paul Cowell/Shutterstock; p8 **tl** Holbox/Shutterstock, p8 **tr** Kletr/Shutterstock, p8 **b** Daniel Petrescu/Shutterstock; p9 **t** Dynamo Limited, p9 **b** nicholas.voisin44/Shutterstock; p10 **t** Krzysztof Odziomek/Shutterstock, p10 **b** Shane Gross/Shutterstock; p11 **t** Jill Lang/Shutterstock, p11 **b** Greg Amptman/Shutterstock; p12 **t** Sergei25/Shutterstock, p12 **b** Studio 37/Shutterstock; p13 **t** Dray van Beeck/Shutterstock, p13 **b** BGSmith/Shutterstock; p14 **t** Amanda Nicholls/Shutterstock, p14 **b** Derek Heasley/Shutterstock; p15 **t** PhotosByChip/Shutterstock, p15 **b** Chad Zuber/Shutterstock; p16 **t** Kletr/Shutterstock, p16 **b** Johannes Kornelius/Shutterstock; p17 **t** aastock/Shutterstock, p17 **b** Tony Campbell/Shutterstock; p18 **t** Vaclav Volrab/Shutterstock, p18 **t** background Dudarev Mikhail/Shutterstock, p18 **b** wonderisland/Shutterstock; p19 **t** Rich Carey/Shutterstock, p19 **b** James A Dawson/Shutterstock; p20 **t** Pat Morris/ardea.com/Shutterstock, p20 **b** Dynamo Limited; p21 **t** Dynamo Limited, p21 **b** Valerie Taylor/ardea.com; p22 **t** Dominique de la Croix/Shutterstock, p22 **b** left Eric Isselee/Shutterstock, p22 **br** Jung Hsuan/Shutterstock; p23 **t** Sergey Skleznev/Shutterstock, p23 **b** Kristina Vackova/Shutterstock; p24 **t** Rich Carey/Shutterstock, p24 **b** wonderisland/Shutterstock, p24 **b** background Dudarev Mikhail; p25 **t** LauraD/Shutterstock, p25 inset stephan kerkhofs, p25 **b** Pat Morris/ardea.com; p26 **t** Cigdem Sean Cooper/Shutterstock, p26 **b** Krzysztof Odziomek/Shutterstock; p27 **t** A Cotton Photo/Shutterstock, p27 **b** Evlakhov Valeriy/Shutterstock; p28 **t** PHB.cz (Richard Semik)/Shutterstock, p28 **b** Jennifer Nicole Buchanan/Shutterstock; p29 **t** frantisekhojdysz/Shutterstock, p29 **b** Dennis Donohue/Shutterstock; p30 **t** serg_dibrova/Shutterstock, p30 **b** leungchopan/Shutterstock

Manufactured in the United States of America
CPSIA Compliance Information: Batch #BW17PK: For Further Information contact Rosen Publishing, New York, New York at 1-800-237-9932.

Contents

Words in **bold** can be found in the glossary on page 31.

What is a fish?

Most fish are **cold-blooded vertebrates**. They live in water, are covered with scales and breathe using gills. However, not all fish obey these rules: tuna are **warm-blooded**, hagfish do not have scales or backbones, lungfish have lungs, and some fish can even walk on land.

fin

scales

gills

This grouper has scales, a backbone, gills and fins.

How fish evolved

Fish appeared about 530 million years ago. They were the first vertebrates on the planet and probably **evolved** from creatures similar to sea squirts (right). The earliest fish looked more like worms, but they had a head that was separate from their tail and a nerve running down the length of their body that would later become the **spinal cord**.

Sea squirts live on the seabed and feed on tiny organisms called plankton. They are often colorful and most are tube- or globe-shaped.

Early fish

Between 500 and 400 million years ago, the world's waters were filled with jawless fish. They were small with flat bodies and no fins, and fed on tiny creatures that they sucked up from the seabed. Their heads were covered with bony armor that protected them from giant **invertebrates** such as sea scorpions. The first bony fish and cartilaginous fish (see p.6) evolved from these jawless fish between 445 and 420 million years ago.

Lampreys are jawless fish that attach themselves to other fish and scrape away their flesh. They are similar to fish that lived 300 million years ago.

Living fossil

In 1938, a South African fisherman pulled a strange fish from the water. Scientists recognized the creature as a coelacanth (pronounced "seel-uh-kanth") – a **species** that people thought had been **extinct** for at least 65 million years. It had fleshy, muscular fins, rather like limbs, and may have been a link in the evolution of fish to four-legged **amphibians** and, eventually, to land animals.

Coelacanths swam in the sea when the dinosaurs were alive. They are deepwater fish that live for up to 60 years.

Classification of fish

There are thought to be more than 32,000 species of fish in the world, but there may be many more yet to be discovered. Fish are **classified** according to the material that makes up their skeletons. Most have skeletons made of bone, but sharks, skates and rays have skeletons made of **cartilage**. Here are some of the many different fish families.

Jawless fish

This group includes lampreys and hagfish. They look like eels and have slimy skin without any scales. Jawless fish first evolved more than 500 million years ago.

Cartilaginous fish

These fish have skeletons made of cartilage instead of bone. They include sharks and rays. Their skin is covered with tooth-like scales that make it feel like sandpaper.

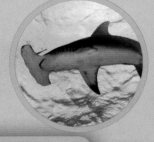

Lobe-finned fish

Coelacanths and lungfish (right) are the only living members of this group of ancient, fleshy-finned fish. **Ancestors** of this group are thought to have evolved into four-legged land animals.

Eels

Eels are long, thin fish. Most are **nocturnal** hunters who live in the shallow waters of the ocean. Some eels are born at sea, but spend most of their lives in freshwater rivers and lakes.

Flatfish

Many of the fish that we eat, including sole and plaice, are flatfish. Both their eyes are on the side of their head that faces upwards as they lie on the seabed, and their skin on this side is **camouflaged**.

Catfish

Catfish are named after their long **barbels**, which look like a cat's whiskers. They are nocturnal and live in freshwater habitats. Some species grow to more than 10 feet (3 m) long.

Cod family

As well as cod, this family includes the haddock, ling, pollack and whiting. These fish are **predators** and most have a barbel on their chin, which they use to search the seabed for food.

Perch family

Perch are freshwater fish that feed on smaller fish, shellfish and insect **larvae**. Some are brilliantly colored. Many species of darters are also members of the perch family.

Sea horses, sea dragons and pipefish

These fish have long snouts and bodies covered with armor-like plates. The male fish in this group takes care of the eggs after the female has laid them, carrying them until they hatch.

Cichlids

This group includes more than 1,600 species. They vary greatly in size and shape, and include wrasse, angelfish and discus fish. All care for their eggs and young, unlike most fish.

Salmon and trout

These fish are predators that feed on smaller fish, shellfish and insects. They are born in freshwater rivers, but many species spend most of their lives at sea, then return to the river to lay their eggs.

Lantern fish

Lantern fish live in the deep sea and have light-producing organs along their body. These light up as they swim and attract the tiny sea creatures that the fish **prey** on.

Sticklebacks

Sticklebacks are named after the spines on their backs. They are related to sea horses and pipefish and have no scales. Males build a nest to attract a female, then guard her eggs once fertilized.

Boxfish

These square-shaped fish include cofferfish, cowfish and trunkfish. They have plate-like scales that form a hard shell, making it difficult for other fish to eat them. They are closely related to puffer fish.

Mackerel and tuna

These fish vary in size from the 8-inch (20-cm) island mackerel to the 15-foot (4.5-m) Atlantic bluefin tuna. Some members of this family are warm-blooded, which helps them to swim at high speed.

Herring and sardines

There are more than 200 species in this family, including many that we like to eat. Most live in the sea and feed on plankton. They swim in large **shoals** that can include millions of fish.

Anatomy of a fish

All fish have heads, **trunks** and tails, but their bodies have evolved differently depending on their lifestyle. Fish that swim in the open ocean are torpedo-shaped and glide through the water. Fish that live among rocks, corals or sea grasses are usually more bulky and slow-moving.

Streamlined tuna are built for speed in open water. Unlike most fish, they are warm-blooded, which gives their muscles extra power.

Boxfish move slowly among coral. They are protected from predators by an armored shell that surrounds their body.

Why do fish have gills?

Fish need oxygen to survive, but most cannot breathe air because they do not have lungs. Instead they swallow water and push it out through their gills. Oxygen from the water passes into the fish's blood as it flows through the gills. At the same time, carbon dioxide passes from its blood through the gills back into the water.

Bright-red feathery gills are found on either side of a fish's neck. This picture shows a close-up of the gills of a giant catfish.

How do fish rise and sink?

Many bony fish have a balloon-like organ called a
swim bladder that they use to keep themselves afloat.
When a fish wants to swim deeper, it lets out oxygen
from its swim bladder. When it wants to go higher, it
fills its swim bladder with more oxygen.

*Scientists
think that the
swim bladder may
have evolved into
the lungs of land
animals.*

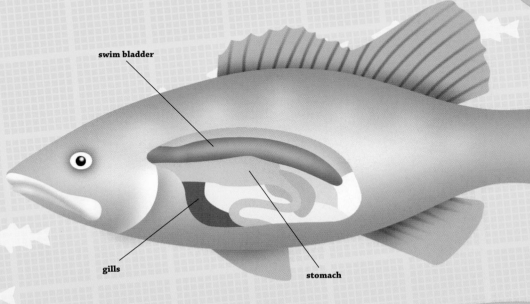

swim bladder

gills

stomach

What are fins for?

Fins are made up of spines
covered with skin. Their main
job is to help a fish to swim.
A fish's tail fin pushes it
forwards through the
water, while its other
fins help it balance,
turn and stop. Some
fish have spines in
their fins that can
inject **venom**.

*The thresher
shark uses its
incredibly long
tail fin to stun or
kill its prey.*

Fish without bones

Sharks, rays and chimaeras have skeletons made from tough, flexible cartilage, which allows these fish to grow to huge sizes. This group of fish includes the enormous whale sharks and manta rays.

Manta rays can grow up to 23 feet (7 m) wide. Other fish often swim alongside these gentle giants to feed on their leftovers.

Sharks

Sharks are among the largest underwater predators alive today. These fierce hunters have excellent hearing and a keen sense of smell, along with razor-sharp teeth that are constantly being replaced. However, the largest sharks are harmless. Whale sharks and basking sharks swim slowly with their mouths open, filtering plankton and other tiny sea creatures from the water.

A hammerhead shark's wide-set eyes give it a better field of view than most predators, while special organs in its head help it to hunt by detecting the electricity generated by its prey.

Skates and rays

These fish have flat bodies and large fins called "wings." Most have mouths and nares (similar to nostrils, seen left between the mouth and the saw) on the underside of their body, and eyes and breathing holes on top of their head. Skates live in cold waters and lay eggs, while rays prefer warm seas and give birth to live young. Most rays have sharp **barbs** on their tail that can inject venom into an attacker.

Sawfish belong to the ray family, although they are also called carpenter sharks.

Chimaeras

We know very little about chimaeras, which include ghost sharks, ratfish, elephant fish and rabbitfish. These strange fish live in the deep ocean, where they feed on shellfish, worms, small fish and jellyfish. Most have a venomous spine on their backs, which they use to defend themselves.

The spotted ratfish lives in the Pacific Ocean. Its long nose is equipped with electrical sensors that can locate shellfish buried beneath the seabed.

Reproduction

Most fish lay eggs, which is called spawning. As the female releases her eggs, a male **fertilizes** them. Many eggs are eaten as they float through the water. Those that survive hatch into larvae, which are still attached to the egg yolk. After a few weeks, they develop into young fish, called fry.

yolk

This newly hatched grouper larva has no mouth. For the next few weeks it will feed on the yolk attached to its stomach.

Caring parents

Most fish abandon their eggs or young, but discus fish care for their babies in the same way that mammals do. While mammals feed their babies on milk, discus fish produce an orange slime on their skin that the newly hatched larvae feed on for the first weeks of their life.

Discus fish live in the Amazon River. After feeding on slime from their parents' skin, these fry become large enough to find their own food.

Role reversal

In the animal kingdom, mothers usually take care of the young, but some fish fathers are dedicated parents. Male sand gobies keep their eggs clean and fan them with their fins. Female sea horses and pipefish lay their eggs inside a pouch on the male's stomach and he carries them until they hatch, while the male cardinal fish protects the eggs by carrying them in his mouth.

The female cardinal fish lays her eggs in the male's mouth. He carries them for about 30 days and cannot eat until they have hatched.

Live birth

Some fish, including most species of shark, give birth to live young. They usually look like miniature adults and are able to hunt for food as soon as they are born. Shark mothers do not care for their young. In fact, the shark pups swim away as quickly as possible, otherwise their mother might eat them!

Baby tiger sharks, such as this one, grow inside their mother's body for up to 16 months.

Senses

Fish use their senses to hunt for food. Most fish have excellent sight and their big, bulging eyes give them a good view of their surroundings. Flatfish begin life with eyes on both sides of their heads, but as they grow, one eye moves until they are both on the upper side of the fish.

The peacock flounder is a flatfish with eyes on little stalks. Its eyes move independently of one another, so the fish can see in all directions.

Smell

Fish use nares (see page 11) for smelling. Sharks have an excellent sense of smell and can detect tiny amounts of blood in the water up to 1.2 miles (2 km) away. Salmon are well known for their sense of smell, which leads them back to the river where they were born, so they can lay their eggs there.

More than half a shark's brain is devoted to its strong sense of smell.

Hearing

A fish's ears are found inside its body, behind its eyes. Sound travels well underwater, so a fish is able to hear noises many miles away. Some fish make sounds using their fins, teeth or by vibrating their swim bladder. This is how they keep in touch with other members of a shoal, attract **mates** or warn of danger.

The toadfish makes a noise like a foghorn when it is eating. This warns other fish to stay away from its food!

lateral line

A unique sense

Some fish have a row of organs along their side that sense movement and vibrations. This is called the lateral line. It stops fish bumping into one another when they swim in a shoal and helps them to find their prey.

This surfperch has a dark lateral line running from its head to its tail.

Freshwater fish

Some fish have evolved to live in freshwater lakes, rivers and streams. Freshwater fish have to cope with greater differences in water temperature than sea fish. There are fewer places for them to escape from predators, so they usually have well-camouflaged skin.

Most catfish live in shallow, running water. They are found in freshwater habitats on every continent except Antarctica.

The turquoise killifish lives for just a few months, but its eggs can survive in the mud for several years.

Fish out of water

Some freshwater fish have evolved ways of surviving if streams and ponds dry up. Lungfish can live without water for up to three years by burrowing into the mud and creating a cocoon of dried slime. Walking catfish can breathe air and walk across land on their fins in search of water. Killifish die at the end of the rainy season but their eggs can survive in a dried-up pond until it rains again. Then, the eggs hatch.

River killers

Rivers are home to some fearsome fish. Piranhas inhabit the waterways of South America and are well known for their razor-sharp teeth. They usually swim in groups and can strip the flesh from an animal in minutes. The Goliath tiger fish, found in the Congo River, Africa, can weigh up to 154 pounds (70 kg) and even attacks small crocodiles. Freshwater stingrays also pack a powerful punch. These well-camouflaged fish grow up to five meters long and have a barb at the base of their tail that injects a deadly poison.

Piranhas have a remarkable sense of smell and a tiny drop of blood in the water will attract them.

Epic journeys

Some fish spend part of their lives in freshwater and part at sea. Salmon are born in a river and swim out to sea, **migrating** vast distances across the ocean. When they are ready to breed, they make the long journey back to the river of their birth. Freshwater eels make the journey in reverse. They are born at sea but spend most of their lives in rivers, returning to the ocean to spawn.

Salmon leap rapids and other obstacles as they struggle to return to their birthplace. They sometimes become easy prey for grizzly bears.

Reef fish

Coral reefs can be home to thousands of species of fish. They have evolved alongside the reef's other inhabitants, such as sharks and anemones, and have developed clever ways of surviving in this crowded habitat.

Many fish that live on reefs have flattened bodies that allow them to hide in narrow spaces.

Parrot of the sea

The colorful parrot fish's tightly packed teeth form a beak, which it uses to scrape **algae** from coral. At night, some parrot fish surround themselves with a protective cocoon, created from slime from their mouths. This may hide their scent from predators while they sleep, and gives them an early warning if the cocoon is touched.

Parrot fish change color as they grow older and females of almost all species can change sex, becoming male if the leading male in the group dies.

A close relationship

Clown fish and sea anemones have evolved together and developed a relationship that helps them both. The clown fish has a protective layer of slime so it can hide among the anemone's stinging tentacles and keep safe from predators. At the same time, it drives away any intruders that come too close to the anemone and keeps its tentacles clean.

The clown fish's bright colors may attract small fish, which are eaten by the anemone.

Cleaner fish

The moray eel hides among rocks and coral and uses its sense of smell to track down prey. Tiny fish would normally be a snack for this fierce predator, but the little cleaner wrasse swims into its mouth quite safely. As it approaches the eel, the wrasse performs a special dance. The eel recognizes this, together with the black stripe on the wrasse's side, and allows the wrasse to remove **parasites** and dead skin from its body.

Cleaner wrasse vibrate their bodies while they are inside a moray eel's mouth to remind it that they are there.

The deep ocean

Until recently, we knew almost nothing about the deepest parts of the ocean and scientists assumed that nothing could live there. However, **submersibles** have discovered undersea vents, which are like hot springs on the ocean floor. These are teeming with life.

Creatures that live around deep-sea vents, such as these tube worms, must survive extreme pressure, high temperatures and poisonous gases.

Life in the midnight zone

Food and mates can be hard to find in the deep ocean and deep-sea fish swim slowly to save energy. The female anglerfish attracts prey with a glowing lure that dangles above her enormous mouth. Her stomach can stretch to hold creatures far larger than she is. Male anglerfish, which are much smaller, use their huge nostrils to sniff out a female. They attach themselves to her with their teeth and their bodies eventually become joined to hers. They feed off the female and, in exchange, they fertilize her eggs.

A female anglerfish may have several male parasites.

Specialized eyes

The barreleye, or spookfish, lives in the deep, dark waters of the Atlantic, Pacific and Indian Oceans. Many deep-sea fish are blind, but the barreleye has a transparent head and barrel-shaped eyes. Its eyes swivel so the barreleye can look up towards the surface of the water to search for the shadows of prey in the dim light. Then it rotates its eyes forwards to home in on its meal.

eye

nare

The barreleye has two nares above its small mouth that are often mistaken for its eyes.

Glowing in the dark

The **bioluminescent** creatures of the deep sea put on a fantastic light show by combining chemicals in their bodies in a similar way to a glow stick. Some fish use their lights like a torch to search for their prey. Others create a bright flash to blind predators.

Flashlight fish have bioluminescent organs beneath their eyes. They use the light to attract prey and for communication.

Deadly creatures

The great white shark is the world's largest and most feared predatory fish, but the oceans are also home to more than 1,000 species of venomous fish that harm about 50,000 people each year.

Humans are much more of a threat to great white sharks than they are to us. Great whites have become endangered as a result of hunting and getting caught in nets.

Double trouble

Puffer fish and porcupine fish move slowly so they are an easy target for predators, but they have evolved two effective ways to defend themselves. If threatened, they fill their stomach with water so that they turn into a spiky ball. If any predator manages to swallow the fish, it will fall victim to the fish's powerful poison.

The long-spined porcupine fish (below, far left) can inflate its body to almost twice its normal size (below). If a shark tries to swallow the fish it may choke.

Beautiful killer

The lion fish's striped fins warn other creatures to keep clear of its venomous spines, which have been known to kill humans. Lion fish are skilled hunters, cornering their prey with their fins and swallowing it whole. They have few predators because of their venom, so their numbers are increasing and threatening the survival of other fish species in the warmer waters of the western Atlantic.

The lion fish's fins are armed with venomous spines.

Hidden danger

The stonefish is one of the most venomous fish in the world, and one of the most dangerous because of its excellent camouflage. It lives in tropical waters, where it usually lies motionless and partly buried, so it looks just like a rock. The stonefish has 13 sharp spines on its back, which each have extremely toxic venom that can kill a human. Thanks to antivenom, deaths are rare nowadays. The last was in Japan in 2010.

It is easy to step on a stonefish because they are so well camouflaged.

Staying alive

Many animals prey on fish, including whales, dolphins, birds and seals, as well as other fish, so fish have evolved ways to protect themselves. About a quarter of fish spend their lives in shoals. By swimming in groups they can confuse a predator and each individual fish is in less danger than if it were alone.

When fish swim in a shoal there are many pairs of eyes to watch for predators.

Taking to the air

Flying fish have many predators including tuna, swordfish and marlin, and they are thought to have evolved their ability to glide through the air as a way of escaping capture. Their streamlined shape helps them to build up speed underwater so they can get airborne.

Flying fish can glide for up to 656 feet (200 m) at a height of more than a 3.3 feet (1 m) on their winglike fins.

Electric organs

Some fish have special organs that can produce an electric charge strong enough to stun prey and scare away predators. They include electric eels (which are actually knife fish, not eels), electric catfish and electric rays.

electric organs

The electric ray has two large electric organs on either side of its head.

A slippery customer

Hagfish have no jaws. They feed on dead and injured sea creatures by slithering inside their bodies and using their rasping tongues to eat them from the inside out. If a hagfish is captured, it produces large amounts of sticky goo that can block the gills of its attacker. This eel-like fish can also tie a knot in its body. This helps the hagfish to escape from predators and, by sliding its body through the knot, it wipes the slime off.

Hagfish live in deep water and have hardly changed since they first appeared on Earth 300 million years ago.

mouth

Extreme fish

Fish range in length from just 0.32 inch (8 mm) to more than 39 feet (12 m). The pygmy goby is not only one of the smallest fish in the world, it also has the shortest lifespan. These tiny reef fish live for an average of just 59 days.

An adult male pygmy goby is just over 0.4 inch (1 cm) long and weighs about four milligrams, or less than one-thousandth of an ounce.

Largest living fish

Whale sharks can reach lengths of more than 41 feet (12.5 m) and weigh more than 23 tons (21 mt). They have teeth, but do not use them. Instead, they scoop plankton and small fish into their huge, gaping mouths as they swim. Sieve-like pads separate the tiny creatures from the water, which the whale shark then pumps out through its gills.

Whale sharks can take in more than 1,585 gallons (6,000 l) of water an hour as they feed.

Speedy hunter

The sailfish is the fastest fish in the ocean, reaching speeds of up to 68 miles per hour (110 km/h). It is named after its huge dorsal fin, which stretches all along its back. This "sail" lies flat while the sailfish is swimming, but the fish raises it when threatened. Groups of fish also use their sails to herd fish or squid together when they are feeding.

The sailfish has a long upper jaw, which juts out to form a spear. This is used to slash or stab prey.

A cold fish

The crocodile icefish lives around Antarctica where the sea temperature drops below freezing. Icefish have clear blood that looks like water because they have no red blood cells. Red blood cells usually move oxygen around the body, but icefish carry oxygen in their blood **plasma** instead. Their blood also contains substances that bind to ice crystals and stop the fish from freezing.

The crocodile icefish has a large heart that beats twice as fast as that of other fish because its clear blood carries less oxygen.

27

The future of fish

Our oceans are so huge it is hard to believe that whole species of fish could disappear. Unfortunately, this could happen because of loss of habitat, pollution, **climate change** and overfishing. Overfishing means that more fish are caught than can be replaced when the fish that are left behind lay their eggs.

Governments are trying to reduce overfishing by banning fishing in certain areas and restricting the amount of fish boats can catch.

Adapting to climate change

Climate change caused by **global warming** affects life in the oceans just as much as on land. Warmer water holds less oxygen than cold water and, as fish need oxygen to grow, in future they could be smaller in size. Some fish are already adapting to warmer temperatures by changing the timing of their migrations.

Salmon have evolved to spawn two weeks earlier in Alaska in response to global warming.

Reefs at risk

Corals are home to small algae, which give the reefs their brilliant colors. When corals are stressed by temperature change or pollution, they shed their algae. This causes coral bleaching and can kill the **colony**. Scientists estimate that global warming and pollution could kill a third of coral reefs in the next 30 years.

About 25 percent of all sea creatures live on coral reefs. There may be many more that we have not even discovered yet.

Evolution through pollution

Between 1947 and 1977, factories along the Hudson River in New York State poured chemicals called PCBs into the water. These dangerous pollutants caused liver tumors in 95 percent of the river's Atlantic tomcod. Some were not affected by the chemicals and survived to breed, so, within 50 years, these fish have evolved to become resistant to PCBs.

This boat, equipped with PCB sensors, is measuring the amount of pollution in the Hudson River.

Fantastic fish

Fish were the first animals with a backbone to live on Earth. Here are just a few of the many amazing facts about some of our planet's oldest inhabitants.

Switching sex
A male emperor angelfish (above) lives with up to five females. If the male dies, one of the females turns into a male and takes over as the leader of the group.

Supersized shark
Megalodon was the biggest shark ever to have lived. It was the size of a bus and its massive jaws could crush a whale's skull. It ruled the oceans between 28 and 1.5 million years ago.

Fish can drown
Fish need oxygen, so if there is not enough oxygen in the water, they will drown.

Slow swimmer
The dwarf sea horse swims so slowly it takes about an hour to travel just 5 feet (1.5 m).

Top tasters
Many species of fish have taste buds on their fins, face and around their tails. Catfish have taste buds all over their bodies. They help the fish to find food in muddy water.

Land-loving fish
The mudskipper (below) walks on its fins and has adapted to spending most of its life on land. It can breathe through the pores of its skin, but only when it is wet, so it carries a supply of water in its gill chambers.

The great unknown
Scientists have explored just one percent of the deepest ocean. They believe there are millions of animals and fish down there, waiting to be discovered.

Glossary

Algae Very simple plants that grow in water

Amphibian An animal that spends part of its life underwater (breathing through gills) and the remainder on land (breathing with lungs)

Ancestor An early type of animal from which others have evolved

Barb A sharp, hook-like spike

Barbel A whisker-like organ that hangs from the mouth of some fish and often has taste buds

Bioluminescent Producing light as a result of a chemical reaction

Camouflage Natural coloring that allows an animal to blend in with its surroundings

Cartilage Flexible tissue, such as that found in human ears and noses

Classify To arrange in groups

Climate change A change in the weather, often thought to be caused by human activity

Cold-blooded An animal whose body temperature changes according to the surrounding air or water temperature

Colony A group of animals of one kind that live close together

Evolve To develop gradually over generations

Extinct When all living members of a species have died out

Fertilize When a sperm from a male animal joins together with an egg from a female to create a new life

Global warming An increase in the temperature of the Earth's atmosphere

Invertebrate An animal without a backbone

Larva The newly-hatched form of a fish or insect

Mate One of a pair of animals that produce young together

Migrating Moving from one area to another according to the seasons, usually to find food

Nocturnal Active during the night

Parasite An animal that lives in or on another creature and feeds on that creature or on its food

Plasma The liquid part of the blood

Predator An animal that hunts other creatures for food

Prey To hunt other creatures for food, or an animal that is hunted by another for food

Shoal A large number of fish, swimming together as a group

Species A group of animals that can breed with one another and produce healthy babies, which are able to breed when they grow up

Spinal cord A bundle of nerves that is enclosed in the spine and connects almost all parts of the body to the brain

Submersible A vehicle designed to operate underwater, often used for research

Trunk The part of the body between the head and tail

Venom A poisonous liquid that creatures inject into their victims

Vertebrate An animal with a backbone

Warm-blooded Able to maintain the same body temperature whatever the temperature of the surroundings

Index

Websites

PowerKids Press has developed an online list of websites related to the subject of this book. This site is updated regularly. Please use this link to access the list:

www.powerkidslinks.com/ww/fish